# *GET* Better *NOT* Bitter

*Turning Hurts and Offenses to Your Advantage*

# YEMI OYINKANSOLA

# GET BETTER NOT BITTER

Turning Hurts and Offenses to Your Advantage
Copyright © 2016 by **Yemi Oyinkansola**

ISBN: 978-1-944652-25-8

Printed in the United States of America. All rights reserved solely by the publisher. This book or parts thereof may not be reproduced in any form, stored in a retrieval system, or transmitted in any form by any means - electronic, mechanical, photocopy. Unless otherwise noted, Bible quotations are taken from the Holy Bible, New King James Version. Copyright 1982 by Thomas Nelson, Inc., publishers. Used by permission.

---

**Published By:**
Cornerstone Publishing
A division of Cornerstone Creativity Group LLC
Info@thecornerstonepublishers.com
www.thecornerstonepublishers.com

---

## Author's Information

For speaking engagement or to order books
by Pastor Yemi Oyinkansola:
Info@yemioyinkansola.com | www.yemioyinkansola.com
+1 510.258.4583

# CONTENTS

Dedication..................................................................6

Acknowledgment......................................................7

Introduction..............................................................9

1. The Pill Of Bitterness........................................13

2. Triggers Of Bitterness.......................................21

3. Is Bitterness The Solution?...............................33

4. What Bitterness Does To You..........................49

5. Decide For Betterment.....................................55

6. Dealing With The Roots Of Bitterness.............75

7. Dominion Over Bitterness................................89

The Greatest Prayer Of A Lifetime........................105

About Pastor Yemi Oyinkansola............................106

# DEDICATION

To my beautiful wife, **Comfort Oyinkansola** and my lovely Children, **Melody and Toluwani.**

To all the faithful members of RCCG Jesus House Antioch California.

To all that are bitter with different experiences of life that will become better persons by reading this book.

# ACKNOWLEDGMENT

I want to first acknowledge the shepherd of my soul, My **Lord and savior Jesus Christ** for saving me from the shackles of the power of sin and the enemy. Thank you Jesus!

This work won't have been possible without the professional and spiritual insight of **Pastor Gbenga Showunmi,** my publisher and his team at Cornerstone Publishing. Your relentless nudging and encouragements made me to be on my toes to put this book together. Your expertise is impeccable.

I want to acknowledge my Parent in the Lord **Pastors Dotun and Floretta Kukoyi**; also my Zonal Coordinator and his dear wife, **Pastors Yinka and Funke Somotun.** I appreciate all the Pastors in CA-2 of RCCG NA and all the workers and ministers at Jesus House Antioch. You all have contributed in making me a better person.

I want to acknowledge my childhood friend **Pastor Isaac Sanusi and his wife** for your love and trust over the years.

I acknowledge my cousin **Dele Oladeji** for accepting me on my first day in the U.S as a student and for all his support.

Finally, I want to acknowledge my staff at Jesus House Antioch. **Mrs Justina Udoh, Mr Jason Pfeiffer and Mrs Juliana Andrews** for your constant supports and sacrifices. Thank you for coping with me to make us better.

# INTRODUCTION

Everyone will, at certain points or the other in their lives, be faced with situations, encounters and experiences that, if not carefully handled, could lead to deep feelings of resentment and bitterness. It is simply inevitable. Ironically, however, while bitterness usually appears natural and justified, the painful repercussions often confirm the contrary – that bitterness is, indeed, a deadly parasite that gradually eats up its host.

To say that bitterness is harmful to our general well-being is an understatement. When we allow bitterness into our lives, we become like a man who deliberately drinks poison and expects his offenders to die. It is never a healthy choice. Bitterness thwarts our relationship with God and man. It destroys our health and leaves us emotionally drained.

Cheeringly, bitterness is a choice, not a must. In other words, not everyone gives in to the tendency to be bitter. In fact, there are many who have successfully converted experiences that should have made them bitter to opportunities for them to be better in all areas of their lives. This is the message that resonates throughout this book.

It is a general fact that life will always try to knock you down through whatever means—people and circumstances—but what happens to you is not as important as how you decide to respond to it. You are the one to decide if you will allow that situation transform you into a bitter or better person. Thankfully, you have several principles and examples from the Scripture on how to handle the offenses, hurts and disappointments of life and turn them to stepping stones for progress and fulfillment of your destiny.

Whatever experience you have gone through or are currently going through, God understands and is able to make all things work together for your good (Romans 8:28). But this can only happen if you willingly surrender your burden of hurts to Him and let Him take charge of the situation for you. He will heal your broken heart and compensate you for all you have endured.

Christ came to give you abundant life, not a life that is fettered physically or emotionally. You were born to be a victor and not a victim in life's circumstances. You must resolve therefore never to allow any experience of life to hinder or subdue the spirit of a conqueror that God has given to you.

In choosing to be better, not bitter, you automatically position yourself to live in true freedom, victory and dominion all the days of your life!

# CHAPTER 1

# THE PILL OF BITTERNESS

◇◇◇◇◇◇◇◇◇◇◇◇◇◇◇◇◇◇◇◇◇◇◇◇◇◇◇◇◇◇◇◇◇◇◇◇◇◇◇

According to Dr. Charles Raison, associate professor of psychiatry at Emory University School of Medicine, once said that "bitterness is a nasty solvent that dissolves everything good." I'm not sure there's a more precise way to describe bitterness. But supposing his illustration is not clear enough to you, let me give it a vivid, personal touch.

Growing up in Africa, especially in my early years, I can still recall how tough it was taking certain medications when I was ill. I knew I needed to take those medications, but the problem was that they had a bitter taste. I remember my mom trying frantically to force some of the liquid medications down my throat. How much I cried. How hard I kicked. How I clenched my teeth. I tell you, it was always a battle.

The point here is that no one likes anything bitter, not even an innocent child. Ever before he is able to discern between good and evil, his tongue is already able to decipher between sweet and bitter. Bitter is that thing which is loathed by all. By implication, therefore, to be described as bitter is to be repulsive, loathsome, unapproachable, overtly sensitive, touchy, extremely resentful, malicious, and vindictive.

No wonder, Psychology Today blogger, Stephen Diamond, Ph.D., defines bitterness as "a chronic and pervasive state of smoldering resentment," and deservedly regards it as "one of the most destructive and toxic of human emotions."

## NATURE OF BITTERNESS

Bitterness has roots. Just like a giant oak tree that has a deep root system that can extend to two or more times its height, bitterness is a deeply and firmly rooted negative emotion. It takes root in the very depths of the human soul. And from there, it has the potency to erupt, causing untold disaster. One writer described it as a root that ruins the garden of peace.

The scriptures confirmed the description of bitterness in Hebrews 12:15-17. There, the example of Esau, the brother of Jacob, is cited. Esau and Jacob, the sons of Isaac and Rebecca, were brothers who had struggled right from the womb (Genesis 25). One day, Esau, a hunter, returned from hunting, famished, and close to dying—at least, that was the idea his empty stomach communicated to his brain. He believed it and asked his brother for a pot of pottage. Jacob who had seen his frustration, decided to play on it.

"Sell me your birth right," he said. Who knows, he might actually have tried that first time to test the waters. But then, famished Esau readily consented. "What is a birth right to a dying man?" he queried. In an instant, he signed a pact that caused him absolute pain for the rest of his life, as it were. We'll talk more about Esau's bitterness of over a decade as we progress.

Now, where are roots found? Roots are found in the ground, sitting beneath the earth's surface. They are the reason trees grow, as they spread their tentacles and take up nutrients from the ground around them to nourish those trees. In the same vein, the root of bitterness in the human soul sucks up affection and compassion from a person's life and replaces it with negative emotions. Bitterness, springing up as a root, magnifies pain, nourishes misery, and amplifies frustration.

# GET BETTER NOT BETTER

## 1. Bitterness Starts Small, Just Like a Seed Sown

Before there is a root, there's first a seed. Seeds are sown in various ways. While humans deliberately put some in the ground, others are carried by the wind; yet others are carried by birds and rodents from one point to another, or by whatever means seeds are dispersed. However, they get sown at some point or other. And then, with a little bit of sunshine here and a little bit of rain there, they begin to germinate.

With much nurturing, the little seed of today soon becomes a herb-sized plant, and then a shrub-sized tree, and then a big tree, which, as long as the roots keep getting nourishment from rain and sunlight, sooner or later begins to produce fruits.

That is the same way it works with bitterness. The tiny seed—a disappointment, a point of disagreement, an act of betrayal—soon blossoms if it is not dealt with. And what it yields as its fruit is everything negative and toxic, at which point it already must have grown into something massive and unmanageable. This is why great caution and wisdom is needed in handling the various encounters and experiences we face in life.

## 2. It Is Unnoticeable to the Eye

You don't see the root of bitterness, and no other

person sees it either. But does the fact that the root is unnoticeable to the human eye make it harmless? Certainly not! In fact, the hidden nature of bitterness makes it even more difficult to deal with. If it were as conspicuous as your face is to everyone who beholds it, then it would be easier for your neighbor to see you and say, 'Hey neighbor, you're bitter. Is anything the matter?'

Again, if it were as open as any other physical part of your body, you'd be able to look in the mirror and identify it at a glance. Sadly, bitterness lies deep down the soil of your soul. And everything you do to nurture it buries it even deeper.

## 3. Bitterness Spreads

Have you ever seen a piece of bread that has mold on it? At first glance, especially at the early stages of the growth of the mold, it appears that the mold is just on one spot. But if you were to look at the piece of bread under a microscope, you would discover long root-like structures spreading through the piece of bread. That's just how bitterness spreads from that point where it begins, often very small and unnoticeable, and moves through your whole being, till it completely ravages it all. What's reflected on the surface isn't exactly what's going on right inside.

Moreover, bitterness spreads from the bitter person to other people around. It spreads very quickly, maybe faster than wild bush fire. A little leaven, scripture says, leavens the whole lump (Galatians 5:6). Have you ever observed how an alarm raised by one person can make a lot of people run helter-skelter, without necessarily knowing what is chasing them? When you allow the root of bitterness, it spreads to everyone in your family, church, neighborhood, indeed everyone around you.

## 4. It Nurtures the Fruits of Evil Speaking and Sedition

The root of bitterness sucks up a person's spiritual and physical energy with which it nourishes the sour grapes of hatred, discontentment, malice, murmuring, irritation, bickering, harsh criticism and evil speaking. It becomes clear that one is full of resentment and bitterness when that person begins to manifest these evil fruits.

And just as plant roots break up clods of soil as they grow ever deeper and gain an ever broader reach, so does the root of bitterness, springing up into these wild vines, compromise unity among human groups (family, church, workplace, neighborhoods, nations) and split apart the best of friends.

## PRAYER POINTS

1. Dear Lord, you who search the reins of the human heart, search me and expose every subtle seed of bitterness.

2. Father of light, beam your light upon my soul and help me recognize bitterness in my heart for what it is and not justify it.

3. Sun of righteousness, let the scourge of your Spirit choke every seed of bitterness in me, lest it becomes a bitter root.

*CHAPTER 2*

# TRIGGERS OF BITTERNESS

◇◇◇◇◇◇◇◇◇◇◇◇◇◇◇◇◇◇◇◇◇◇◇◇◇◇◇◇◇◇◇◇◇◇◇◇◇◇◇◇

In the previous chapter, I mentioned it briefly that bitterness begins as a seed, which could have been sown in a number of ways. I consider it necessary that we now explore these various catalysts of bitterness. The reason for this is threefold. One, it is an established fact that no physician can recommend an effective cure for a disorder without first diagnosing its true nature and cause. This is especially important because, sometimes, some people can't explain why they're perpetually bitter and temperamental.

Secondly, even for those who have an idea of the root cause of their bitterness, I believe this exploration will prove to be a form of catharsis, which will help to confirm that they are not alone and therefore can triumph over the grip of bitterness on their lives.

Thirdly, it may help us in understanding why some individuals tend to manifest traits that are symptomatic of the roots of bitterness. This, however, is not an attempt at justifying bitterness or any of its various manifestations (I will dwell more on this in the succeeding chapters). It is simply to provide enlightenment that could equip and position us to be potential sources of help to bitter people, rather than being aggravators of their plights through wrong reactions.

## 1. Abuse

One of the most common avenues through which Satan sows the seed of bitterness in people's lives is abuse. When someone has experienced or witnessed abuse, it is easy for them to become bitter, not just towards the abuser but anyone that shares similar physical, racial or even religious traits with them.

Abuse has been described as "an attempt to control the behavior of another person. It is a misuse of power which uses the bonds of intimacy, trust, and dependency to make the victim vulnerable." Abuse could be **physical,** in which a person is bullied, hit (kicked, slapped, punched, etc.), or threatened with a weapon. It could be **sexual,** in which the victim is forced to engage in unwanted, non-consensual sex in any form. This obviously includes rape—date rape, marital rape, birth rape, acquaintance rape, rape by strangers. Abuse could also be **verbal**, which involves constant criticism, hurtful name-calling, harsh put-downs, and repeated blaming and threatening. It could also be **emotional or psychological,** in which a person is discriminated against and made to feel worthless and inferior through deprivation, stigmatization, and isolation.

In whichever way abuse is meted out, it has the potential to seriously interfere with an individual's emotional development and over time, can cause significant detriment to their self-esteem, emotional well-being, physical state, and worst of all, their outlook towards life and relationship with others. It becomes more complicated when the abuse is perpetrated by a parent, close relative, a trusted individual or someone who seems untouchable, either because of the position they occupy or because of the reputation they have.

## 2. Circumstances of Birth or Family Situation

For many, bitterness springs from the history of their birth or the perpetual hardship or crisis in their family. There are people who have been told that they were born of incest or rape. And there are those who have been told that their birth was a mistake or who have discovered that their real parents actually abandoned them at birth.

There are those who have been orphaned very early in life, and, worse still, abandoned by relatives. And then, there are those whose parents are alive but whose families seem to be dysfunctional. Parents are either too busy to care or they are in the thrall of some addiction (to alcohol, to hard drugs, to pornography, etc.). Or the parents could be continually bickering or always in and out of jail.

It's also possible that the parents are divorced, with each parent being horribly bitter towards the other and joint custody becomes a terrible struggle. Children in or from such homes often wonder how things degenerated by degrees to such point of dysfunctionality. Such children may become bitter against their parents for not working a little harder to make their marriage work.

But then, there are families that are relatively stable. Their only problem is poverty. Have you ever seen such abject poverty where families struggle to feed daily? There are people born into such families and they keep wondering why. Even the basic necessities of life seem completely out of their reach. They are familiar with hunger pangs. The result, sometimes, is a life of bitterness.

## 3. Delays and Disappointments

Some people become bitter through repeated failures, delays and disappointments in life. It could be in their career pursuits or business investments. It could be in getting married or in getting the fruit of the womb. After series of let-downs and downturns, the tendency to become bitter grows. This gets even more complicated when there are others around who seem to be succeeding and everything seems to be working just fine in their lives. If care is not taken, jealousy begins to fester along.

I think the area where this trigger of bitterness gets easily entrenched and effective is in the area of relationship. Consider this scenario. You have a good job, a family that loves you, parents that dote on you, friends that adore you. But more than these, you need a special someone. But for some inexplicable reasons, that special someone comes and before long things go awry between you both. You cannot exactly place your finger on it. You cannot say this or that is the reason this relationship cannot work. You move from one disappointing relationship to another. And just when you are about to give up the idea of ever having that special someone in your life, another knight in shining armor comes along and sweeps you right off your feet.

This time you are confident you have reached your final rest. He asks that you take him to see your parents. He asks for you to go with him to visit his. No other man has come that close to marrying you. Soon, in a fairy tale manner, he asks you to spend the rest of your life with him. You are ecstatic. You are the happiest woman on earth and beyond. Wedding preparations begin in earnest. Suddenly, your prince charming begins to drag his feet. At first, it seemed like just the normal cold feet people develop when they about to take a big step like walking down the aisle.

You are patient with him. You try to empathize. But gradually, reality begins to set in. the man who could not live a day without you is suddenly growing cold on you. It begins to get clearer. He wants out, but is afraid to say it. You take the bold step. You'd rather stage the walkout than have another man make a fool of you. So, you confront him. He says nothing. You tell him you're calling off the engagement. He shrugs. No pleading. No explanation. No apologies. Just like that. You are jolted out of your fairy tale dream. It's over. For the umpteenth time, you have been used and dumped by yet another man.

For many, this is where the root of bitterness against God and against humanity begins.

## 4. Perceived Societal Aberrations and Injustices

This is very common with people from disadvantaged societies and communities. In many African countries, for example, there is so much discontent and bitterness, especially as people contrast what they experience and witness in their society with the picture they get about living conditions in other developed parts of the world. Frustrations and, ultimately, bitterness sets in.

Let me give you another illustration. A man has been content, or at least at ease with his environment. Then he has reasons to go to a neighboring environment. The order that greets him, the beauty, the splendor, is a far cry from what he knows back home. He suddenly becomes angry about the way things are in his own community. He is further infuriated when he begins to see that his own community is better positioned to provide a better life for its people. But that's not the case. If care is not taken, what ensues is bitterness.

There are those whose concern is not socio-economic backwardness of their society but the prevalence of injustice. Such people hate injustice; they hate to see the poor and defenseless being trampled upon. But the oppressors are everywhere and there is little or nothing the concerned individual can do to help the situation. This kind of feeling has driven many into a perpetual state of bitterness. It has made some take a stance against God, the law, authorities and everything they perceive as promoting injustice.

It is said of the late Steve Jobs, for example, that he declared that he wanted nothing to do with God or religion anymore when he spotted a shocking cover photo on "Life" magazine at age 13. The picture displayed a pair of starving children during the Nigerian civil war (1967-1970).

## 5. The Mystery of Natural Disasters, Diseases and Deformities

Every day, reports of terrible natural disasters, accidents and horrible diseases are released by the media. This really vexes certain people to the extreme. They just don't get it. Why do such things happen?

You're the worst hit when a loved one is on a plane that disappears. You're still trying to understand why God would allow floods, hurricanes, earthquakes, landslides, ocean surges, and famines; even though they bring about untold suffering and pain to the world He created. And then you realize that there are diseases everywhere – cancers, Ebola, Zika virus – some of which affect seemingly innocent people, especially children.

There are also children born with deformities. Some people consider such happenings and are deeply frustrated. This frustration, if not dealt with, degenerates into bitterness in the long run.

## 6. Disabilities

There are people who wish to do so much in life but feel so incapacitated by disabilities. Such disabilities could be congenital or through some life-altering mishaps. For many in this category, the feelings of powerlessness and the discomforts of having to depend on others for certain aspects of daily living is sometimes allowed to degenerate into bitterness.

As someone has rightly observed, "for many people, chronic illness/disability is not a short-term inconvenience but rather a long-term, often permanent way of life. In the early stages of adaptation, the changes that happen in our lives and families may seem tolerable—at least while we still think there is a chance that the diagnosis is wrong or the cure is in the magic pipeline offered by big pharmacy. Eventually, denial and bargaining give way to anger and depression. The uninvited guest is still ever-present, and no amount of cajoling or suggestions result in change. Bouts of anger may become a way of life for a while..."

## 7. Offenses

Sometimes, the root of bitterness may not be as deep and repeated as all the previously mentioned triggers. For some, it could just be a wrong done to them, which the wrongdoer has either refused to admit or apologize for. Acts of disrespect, cheating, fraud, slander, spreading false rumors etc., can fester for so long in the mind that it leads to bitterness.

Now, having considered all the reasons for which many people often give in to bitterness, the question is: Is bitterness really the solution to any of these issues or does it contain the answer to any of the questions that often bother the minds of people? Let's delve deeper into this.

## PRAYER POINTS

1. Father of all wisdom, give me the wisdom I need to handle the various encounters and experiences I'm faced with in life.

2. Master of all circumstances, please speak peace to every circumstance in my life, which is capable of banishing me into the dark abyss of bitterness.

3. Faithful Friend and Father, I commit this unpleasant

situation (you can mention the specific challenge you are going through) I ask that it will not plant a seed of bitterness in me, that I will not see my challenges as a moral justification to be bitter.

*CHAPTER 3*

# IS BITTERNESS THE SOLUTION?

◇◇◇◇◇◇◇◇◇◇◇◇◇◇◇◇◇◇◇◇◇◇◇◇◇◇◇◇◇◇◇◇◇◇◇◇◇◇◇◇◇

My simple and honest answer to this is NO. I am sorry if you feel a little disappointed by this response; but while it is true that we can sometimes believe we have justifiable reasons to be bitter, a closer look at what we get from being bitter will make us shudder and have a rethink.

To say it simply, in resorting to bitterness as a way of dealing with life's difficulties, we are simply digging up a bigger hole to fill up another. You will have a better understanding of what I mean by this as we consider, in this chapter and the next, the terrible devastations that bitterness can cause to your relationship with God and fellow men, as well as the destructive effects it can have on you as a person.

## HOW BITTERNESS AFFECTS YOUR RELATIONSHIPS

Bitterness, apart from exposing its victim to all sorts of health problems, is also capable of making them very repulsive people who are unable to maintain any productive relationship. Bitterness destroys any kind of relationship, be it in your marriage, at work, church, or even social setups.

Bitterness poisons your personality with negativity, such that you're blinded to the positive traits in other people. You're just an impossible person to live with, because all you see in people around you is negativity. Bitterness makes you an extremely toxic person that no human being desires to be around.

A bitter wife will be a bickering wife. It is impossible to have a healthy marriage relationship if either of the spouses is a sack of bile, for nothing his or her partner does will work to please the bitter spouse. There isn't one marriage where the spouses do nothing to hurt each other. But bitterness only manifests when you hold onto hurts and refuse to forgive the person who hurt you. Each offense takes residence in the heart, and at some point there is no more room left. That's when bitterness causes the most damage.

Many marriages have hit the rocks owing to the operation of this bitter root in the lives of the couples. And the sad thing is that they just watched while that happened, completely helpless and unable to save their marriage.

The presence of bitterness in the home doesn't stop at destroying the marriage relationship alone. The children that such marriage produces also stand the risk of being destroyed. Children, by nature, are very sensitive to conflict between their parents. While disagreement is normal in any family, a continuation of conflict makes life very difficult for children.

It is impossible for children to enjoy their parents when there is lingering bitterness and bickering between such parents, particularly if they put the children in the middle of the conflict. This puts a lot of stress (emotional, psychological and even physical stress) on the children, and in the long run, it makes them withdrawn and shy, with a low sense of self-worth. And, soon, they start having problems with their studies. A child, who had once been bright academically, now begins to struggle. He moves from being at the top of his class to the bottom.

Your child's development can be seriously hampered by exposure to hostility, violence, resentment and bitterness. Many of the street urchins, pick-pockets, drug addicts, armed robbers, and so on, that you are wary of are only products of homes where hatred and bitterness is the order of the day.

How about your relationship with neighbors and people you daily interact with? As I said before, bitterness destroys any kind of relationship you can think about. You can never make a good neighbor to anyone if bitterness rules your heart. Every space you share, the car park, driveway, will be incomparably smaller than a bucket; it will never be enough for you and any other person because you're so irritable and short-tempered.

How about relationships with your colleagues at the workplace? It is very sour because bitterness in your life has taken the better of you; you become so critical of others' works to the point of making them lose their job. If you're the boss, you make life unbearable for your subordinates. You have zero-tolerance for people; you cannot tolerate little shortcomings. You hire and fire at will because nobody is good enough for you. Those who don't understand call you a perfectionist, when in reality; you're being plagued by bitterness.

In church, you're perpetually bitter towards your pastor because you think his messages are a direct attack on your personality. Your pastor, if he doesn't have a backbone, deliberately begins to sift his sermons because he is afraid of hurting you anymore than he already has. Members of the church suffer from your toxicity. Every rumor begins from your lips. Every gossip emanates from you. Contention in families is brought on by something toxic you said to someone's wife about her husband. You spread hate, distribute chaos, and many brethren are weary because you are present in that local assembly.

If you're a pastor's wife, it makes their burden even greater, because you're at the hem of affairs. You usurp your husband's authority and trample on other leaders, simply because of bitterness. You make it difficult, nay, impossible for the Holy Spirit to move in the church because the Spirit of God cannot thrive where there is strife, occasioned by bitterness.

## YOUR RELATIONSHIP WITH GOD

Above all, bitterness affects your relationship with God. First and foremost, if you are not yet a child of God, bitterness makes it impossible for you to become one. The reason is not far-fetched. Bitterness takes up every space in your heart, so much so that it becomes extremely impossible for you to receive God's love. And since you cannot open your heart to receive God's love, you continue to wallow in bitterness and sin.

Let's even say you're a child of God and somehow you allow bitterness to take root in your heart, any chance for spiritual growth will be stifled. As long as you continue to dwell in the past, what people did to offend you and such likes, you will never be able to attain to higher spiritual heights. And before long, your relationship with God will be ill-affected. You will relapse completely into sin.

Bitterness will render your prayers, services and even offerings unacceptable to God. This is so serious that Jesus emphatically said, **"Therefore if you bring your gift to the altar, and there remember that your brother has something against you, leave your gift there before the altar, and go your way. First be reconciled to your brother, and then come and offer your gift. Agree with your adversary quickly, while you are on the way with him, lest your adversary deliver you to the judge, the judge hand you over to the officer, and you be thrown into prison"** (Matthew 5:23-25).

Need I say that bitterness will rob you of eternity with God in heaven? Yes, and this is the most destructive blow of bitterness. Heaven is such a holy place that nothing filthy or toxic can enter into it. If death meets you harboring bitterness against anyone, whether for "justifiable" reasons or not; or if Jesus suddenly returns and bitterness still clogs your heart, the load of bitterness will make it impossible for you to walk the narrow way that leads to heaven, and the very heavy weight of bitterness will make it impossible for you to fly at the trumpet's sound.

In summary, most of what I have mentioned in this chapter, an author has listed the following reasons why God will not condone bitterness among His children:

- It is an inability to love God. If we fail to forgive, we break the commandments of the loving God.
- It creates an emotional focus toward the one who hurt us. This focus results in us becoming just like the one we resent.
- It hinders prayer, since it is sin. 1 Peter 3:7.
- It retains the sins of the past, brings them into your present state.
- It affects your future and your relationships with others.

- It can make you a stumbling block to those around you.

- It causes division in the body of Christ.

- It gives Satan the advantage over your life.

## DANGERS OF BITTERNESS

Let me show you some examples from the Scripture that clearly portray what bitterness can cause to your relationship with others.

### 1. Murder Through Bitterness (Genesis 4)

You remember Adam and Eve bore children after the fall and their eventual eviction from the Garden of Eden? Of course, you also know what necessitated the fall. The first man and woman disobeyed God's command not to eat the fruit from a particular tree. The children born to the couple immediately after the fall were Cain and Abel.

The fall brought about sin and depravity. So, it didn't come as a surprise when, as a result of bitterness and envy, Cain killed his brother, Abel. Cain's reason for being bitter against his brother was quite unreasonable. This is it. Cain and Abel were both farmers; at least that's how we'll regard them today. While Cain was a food crop farmer, Abel was a livestock farmer.

Now, both of them were expected to offer a part of whatever they got from their farms to God. While Abel offered the fattest animal in his flock, Cain offered the leanest crops from his farm. Expectedly, God was pleased with the sacrifice of Abel more than He was with that of Cain. Who wouldn't be?

I still wonder many times, why didn't Cain just improve his sacrifice to God? Why didn't he, like Abel, his brother, sacrifice the best of his harvests? Rather than do the same thing his brother did to gain God's pleasure and approval, he allowed his envy of his brother degenerate into the bitter root, until he finally convinced himself that taking his brother's life was the only way he could get himself God's approval again. But what did he gain instead? God's displeasure and wrath!

We never can tell, maybe Cain even reckoned that if he killed Abel, God would be forced to appreciate him and his lean sacrifices. Whatever his reasons for killing his brother, one thing is clear, he was blinded by his bitterness.

## 2. Bitterness Produces Irrational Behavior

The story of King Saul's hatred towards David is

quite familiar. He obstinately persecuted David simply because he felt his popularity was waning, while David's praise was being sung by everyone in Israel. He did everything he could to kill David. So blinding was his bitterness that he forgot that David was the only one that could skillfully play the harp which helped to banish his frequent bouts of depression. Never did it occur to him that if he had succeeded in killing David in one of his attempts on his life in the palace, he himself would have died of the torments of depression.

Saul's bitterness against David got to a point that his own children also bore the brunt of it. Jonathan who happened to be a very good friend to David almost found himself in a position where he had to choose between his father (the guilty one) and David (his innocent friend). Things got so bad that Saul even attempted to kill his own son for supporting David.

### 3. Bitterness and Self-ruin

Haman is a classic example of someone who allowed himself to be blinded by bitterness to his own destruction. His name crops up in the Book of Esther.

The king, Ahasuerus, had just elevated Haman and he wanted badly for everyone around to acknowledge that and pay obeisance to him. One day, as he passed by the king's guards' court, everyone, but Mordecai, Esther's uncle (I'm sure you remember her. She was the beautiful devout Jewess, who became the wife of Ahasuerus, the king) and a loyal royal official would not bow in obeisance to him.

Now, you must understand that Mordecai's refusal to bow to Haman wasn't born out of spite for his person or position. Rather it was in obedience to God's word. The simple fact of the matter was that Haman was an Amalekite and God had declared perpetual war on the Amalekites (see Exodus 17:16).

Not minding the consequences, devout and reverential Mordecai chose to obey God rather than men. Risking great danger both to himself, his ward, Esther and the entire Jewish race, he maintained his integrity by refusing to bow to one against whose entire generation the God of Israel had declared perpetual war. In retaliation for Mordecai's perceived insubordination, Haman sought not only to destroy Mordecai as an individual, but cooked up a huge conspiracy to annihilate the entire Jewish race.

Imagine that! One man has offended you and you think it necessary to wipe out an entire generation in your quest for retributive justice? That's what Haman set out to do, forgetting that it is a hard thing to fight against God's own chosen people. He probably was too blinded by bitterness, or too ignorant to recall that in Bible history, no one had ever pitched camp against God's elect and won.

If Haman had not allowed himself to be unnecessarily blinded to the truth on ground; if he had for an instant tried to recall the importance of the Jewish race in God's scheme of events; if he had allowed himself to live past his desire for revenge and had heard the voice of wisdom from his subordinates; if he had not allowed the poison of bitterness to erode his senses, he most definitely wouldn't have ended the way he did.

Now, had Haman been able to follow through with this plan of genocide, all the Jews would have been wiped out at this crucial juncture in history. The promised Seed of the woman would not have been able to come into the world, and the redemption plan would have been altogether foiled. While Haman thought that he was fighting Mordecai and the Jews, he was actually fighting against the True and Living God. He was fighting against his Maker. Have you ever seen any who took the battle to God and prevailed?

I'm certain that if Haman had not been so taken up by the bitter root, he would have been able to rationalize things as they really were. He would have understood that fighting against the Jews was a direct confrontation to the God of all flesh. The tables soon turned. Haman ended up in the same gallows he had prepared for Mordecai. Doesn't this portray bitterness as the concoction we prepare for the destruction of others and end up consuming ourselves?

## 4. With Bitterness, There Are No Sacred Boundaries!

Herodias has been described by some people as one of the wicked women of the Bible (next to Jezebel). She became the wife of Herod Antipas after divorcing Philip I, who was a half-brother to Herod Antipas. It was by Antipas that she had a daughter, Salome, whom she used to kill John the Baptist.

What was John's offense? As a messenger of God, he had the obligation to correct Herod and Herodias for their adulterous relationship. Herodias was bitter about this and patiently waited for an opportunity to get even. It wasn't enough that Herod had had John detained, Herodias wanted more. But why not do it herself? Why use a child?

How was she able to pull that off? Apparently, Herodias knew Herod only too well. He was a man given to sensuality. So, as his birthday approached, she masterfully hatched her nefarious plot to destroy John the Baptist. While they wined to no end, she used her own daughter to excite and arouse Herod's passions. She would stop at nothing to carry out her plan, and that included sacrificing her child's modesty in order to make Herod succumb to her will and do her bidding.

Herod, who was remotely overcome by Salome's form (as revealed by the seductive clothing her mother adorned her in) and immediately taken in by her nimbleness in dancing, a skill which I imagine her mother had helped her acquire as part of her game plan, took a rash and foolish oath to give her whatever she asked, even to half of his kingdom. What would a girl do with up to half of Herod's kingdom, for crying out loud? Thus, in one moment of ecstatic euphoria, he gave the daughter of scheming Herodias a blank check and put his seal on it.

Approaching her mother, Salome inquired of her, "What shall I ask?" Without a moment's hesitation, bitter, revenge-seeking Herodias replied, "Ask for the head of John the Baptist." She didn't have to think about anything at that moment. She had it all thought out.

In an instant, she had snatched the childhood of an innocent girl. That dastardly act would no doubt linger in the conscience of that child for a very long time, perhaps for the rest of her living years. By the way, what did Herodias need John's head in a charger for? Absolutely nothing! She just had to get rid for him after nursing those bitter feelings for so long.

I'm sure you would definitely agree with me that bitterness, in each of these instances, never led to anything good. Like a loose cannon, all it spread about were bullets of death and devastation. And if you nurse bitterness in your heart, do you think the result would be different. Wouldn't you rather deal with that bitterness than allow it ruin everything and everyone that is dear to your heart? Wouldn't you rather deal with it than allow it rob you of God's love and ultimately, heaven?

But in case you're thinking that the effect of nursing bitterness is only destructive to others, then you may need to have a rethink. The poison of bitterness does much more harm to the carrier than it does to the receiver. Let's see how!

## PRAYER POINTS

1. Heavenly Father, protect me from every attack driven by bitterness.

## GET BETTER NOT BETTER

2. Balm of Gilead, heal every heart, marriage, or relationship that I may have hurt through bitterness.

3. Eternal Father, in your mercy, do not allow this cankerworm to prevent me from spending eternity with you in heaven.

*CHAPTER 4*

# WHAT BITTERNESS DOES TO YOU

◇◇◇◇◇◇◇◇◇◇◇◇◇◇◇◇◇◇◇◇◇◇◇◇◇◇◇◇◇◇◇◇◇◇◇◇◇◇◇◇◇◇◇◇

Someone rightly said that bitterness is a concoction we create for someone else, but end up drinking ourselves. It is like cancer that completely ravages the human body. This reminds me of a story I read in the book, The Biblical Guide to Alternative Medicine, by Dr. Michael Jacobson and Dr. Neil T. Anderson. It centers on a pastor's wife in Ohio, USA. She was said to have been diagnosed of stage four of breast cancer, which had metastasized to her entire body. If you know anything about the disease, you'll know for sure that at that stage, it's irreversible. But then, in response to the diagnosis, this woman was said to have gone, in the company of her husband, to seek the counsel of a Georgian pastor and mentor. After the session, they agreed that she had to free her life of any form of emotional poison.

And, yes, she did have someone she had held a grudge against for so long. She let go of that, forgave the woman, and before long, she began to heal. It was simply miraculous. A woman who had been condemned to die, came alive. And she lives on years after the doctors declared she had only a few weeks more to live.

Today, if you were to ask her, Candice would say that the most powerful, physical healing agent available is not a drug, it is a sound, healthy spiritual mind and heart. Having survived one of the most ravaging diseases, not by any medication, she now truly appreciates the healing power of God, and of course, the healing power of a mind free of toxicity.

A 2001 quote from Dr. Colbert says, "While nutrition, vitamins and lifestyle changes are critically important in preventing cancer and helping us through cancer, it is important to deal with such negative emotions as bitterness, resentment, unforgiveness, hatred, guilt and shame, which actually cause the body to produce toxic material. They also increase cortisol levels, which in turn weakens the immune system…"

The Scripture aptly asks an instructive question in Proverbs 6:23: **"Can a man take fire to his bosom, And his clothes not be burned?"** Bitterness, like a fire, while seemingly meant to destroy another person will certainly do more harm to the one nursing it within. The ironical thing is that the supposed cause or target of the bitter feelings may just be going about their normal activities, while the bitter person continues to die within and hindering their own progress in life.

In his book, *Guiding your family in a misguided world*, Dr. Anthony T. Evans, in trying to drive home the effect that holding on to a negative past can have on one's progress in all areas of life, told a very interesting story.

According to him, one day, two monks were walking through the countryside. They were on their way to another village to help bring in the crops. As they walked, they spied an old woman sitting at the edge of a river. She was upset because there was no bridge, and she could not get across on her own. The first monk kindly offered, "We will carry you across if you would like." "Thank you," she said gratefully, accepting their help. So the two men joined hands, lifted her between them and carried her across the river. When they got to the other side, they set her down, and she went on her way.

After they had walked another mile or so, the second monk began to complain. "Look at my clothes," he said. "They are filthy from carrying that woman across the river. And my back still hurts from lifting her. I can feel it getting stiff." The first monk just smiled and nodded his head.

A few more miles up the road, the second monk complained again, "My back is hurting me so badly, and it is all because we had to carry that silly woman across the river! I cannot go any farther because of the pain." The first monk looked down at his partner, now lying on the ground, moaning. Then he asked him a thought-provoking question: "Have you wondered why I am not complaining?" When the complaining monk shook his head to answer in the negative, his partner told him bluntly: "Your back hurts because you are still carrying the woman. But I set her down five miles ago."

Isn't this a poignant lesson? The reason, many people, like the second monk seem to be perpetually bothered and burdened is because they just cannot let go of the past. And as it's obvious from the story, it's just self-inflicted punishment. The woman that the monk was complaining about as the cause of his misery and impeded progress had long continued with her life but the monk remained fettered emotionally and thus miserable on the outside.

It may surprise you to know that more heart-related problems are triggered by negative emotions. In fact, one expert noted that "The data that negative mental states cause heart problems is just stupendous. The data is just as established as smoking, and the size of the effect is the same."

Lovers of classical music must know the name Beethoven. It's a household name in the world of music. For nearly two centuries, the cause of this famous musician's death was a mystery. In 1994, two Americans launched a study to determine the cause of Beethoven's death. Chemical analysis of a strand of his hair showed that he had died of lead poisoning. The poison very possibly took its toll on his system little by little until it killed him.

The poison that killed Beethoven could have come from his drinking out of cups lined with lead or taking his meals on a lead-lined dish – both common household items in his day. It might also have come from eating contaminated fish or even excessive consumption of wine. The point is that the poisoning didn't happen at once. The lead killed him slowly and steadily – one little bit of poison at a time.

This is the same effect that bitterness has upon its

carrier. It kills them little by little. This was why Joyce Meyer, author of the inspirational book, Power of the Mind, once said, "I know from personal experience how damaging it can be to live with bitterness and unforgiveness. I like to say it's like taking poison and hoping your enemy will die. And it really is that harmful to us to live this way." As we will soon see, Joyce Meyer more than had her fair share of abuse, first, by her father and later husband, but she didn't allow herself to be consumed by bitterness. This is the same decision I invite you to take as we consider the next chapter.

## PRAYER POINTS

1. Faithful Father, please uproot every root of bitterness weighing on me and causing defilement.

2. My Healer, my Helper, heal me of every hurt I have brought upon myself by allowing bitterness take root in my heart and life.

3. Gentle Savior, bind my broken heart and heal my relationship with You. Bring me back to Yourself, as I begin the walk from bitterness to betterment.

*CHAPTER 5*

# DECIDE FOR BETTERMENT

◇◇◇◇◇◇◇◇◇◇◇◇◇◇◇◇◇◇◇◇◇◇◇◇◇◇◇◇◇◇◇◇◇◇◇◇◇◇

There is a popular saying that if life throws lemons at you, all you need do is make lemonade out of them. Triggers of bitterness, such as offenses, disappointments and hurts are an inescapable part of life. But not everyone gets subdued by such experiences to the point of bitterness. There are many who choose, instead, to become better through the darts of disappointments that life shoots at them.

The implication is that bitterness is a choice. You can choose to be better, rather than being bitter. In this chapter, I'll be showing you people in contemporary times and in the Bible, who chose to be better despite challenging situations, and how that singular decision changed the course of their lives for the best.

## UNFAZED BY ABUSE

I have decided to open this chapter with a compelling story I read somewhere about a young black man, whose sensibilities were abused from a very young age.

Kevin Benton had every reason to feel bitter. According to him, during his sophomore year in college, white students harassed him and the only other African-American living on the floor in his dorm in order to get them to move out.

The white students spat on their doors, tore their posters off the wall, and banged on their door at four in the morning. When Benton brought up the problems at a dorm meeting, the other students snickered.

"I felt like I was being bullied, being targeted," he says now of his college experience 19 years ago. "I knew I couldn't retaliate in any way or I'd lose my basketball scholarship."

This was the first time in his life Benton had encountered racism and it hit him hard. He had trouble sleeping, and then over the next several months he suffered panic attacks. Admitted to the hospital, he was found to have hypertrophic cardiomyopathy or thickening of the muscles in the heart. The disease is the leading cause of heart-related sudden death in people under 30.

So sick he couldn't walk, Benton lay in his hospital bed bitter and resentful.

"I thought to myself, 'I've never hurt anybody. I serve in the community. I work with youth. I wrestled with God - why did this happen to me?'" he recalled.

Just then, a janitor walked by and grabbed Benton's hand, and prayed aloud to God to heal him. "As soon as she said, 'Amen,' I felt like someone had poured cold water on my head and made my heart shrink," he says.

That day, Benton forgave the students who had tormented them, and three days later, he walked out of the hospital. "If I hadn't forgiven them, I'd be dead," says Benton, now healthy and a social worker for the Philadelphia Department of Human Services.

## SOARING AMIDST VICTIMIZATION

If there was anyone who should have justifiably been bitter all through life, it should have been Joseph. He suffered abuse and injustice like no other person. He was ridiculed, victimized, ostracized, dehumanized, blackmailed, unjustly imprisoned and abandoned by people he trusted and helped. Through it all, he refused to be bitter against anyone. He chose betterment, instead.

In fact, his father, in describing him said, **"Joseph is a fruitful bough, a fruitful bough by a well; his branches run over the wall. The archers have bitterly grieved him, shot at him and hated him. But his bow remained in strength, And the arms of his hands were made strong by the hands of the Mighty God of Jacob (From there is the Shepherd, the Stone of Israel)... The blessings of your father have excelled the blessings of my ancestors, up to the utmost bound of the everlasting hills. They shall be on the head of Joseph, and on the crown of the head of him who was separate from his brothers"** (Genesis 49:22-27).

So, what was the story of Joseph and why is it so instructive and inspiring? He was a motherless child, who was a greatly beloved child of his father. He had dreams of becoming great someday, which he often shared with his brothers. His brothers grew envious of him and decided to kill him. By divine intervention however, they changed their mind and decided to sell him off to a strange land. While in the strange land, he served as a house-keeper. He was dutiful and ever bubbly. While trying to settle down and forget about the ill-treatment of his brothers, his master's wife began to do all she could to seduce him. When he refused, she lied against him that he had tried to rape her. All his explanations and entreaties fell on deaf ears and his master cast him into prison.

Even in prison, Joseph refused to be bitter. He remained active and optimistic. Rather than being bitter, he chose to make the lives of others better. In the process, he helped two other prisoners interpret their dreams. Things happened according as he had predicted and he told the one that was to be restored to the king's palace to remember him. Again, he was dealt a cruel blow, as the man got so excited and self-centered that he completely forgot about Joseph.

It was two years later when the king, Pharaoh, had a dream that no one could interpret, that the man remembered Joseph. Still, when he was called for the interpretation, Joseph did not allow the wrong done to him in the past to prevent him from doing good. He went on to interpret Pharaoh's dream and he was made the Prime Minister of Egypt.

In the course of time, a great famine came upon the

entire region, affecting not only Egypt, but also Israel where Joseph's family was. Thankfully, as Joseph had foreseen the famine, he had ordered that plenty of food be stored for good seven years in Egypt. And when the famine began, he was placed in charge of selling the food to the people. When Joseph's brothers heard that there was plenty of food for sale in Egypt, they decided to try their luck. Since they couldn't recognize Joseph again, they came to him. Fortunately, he could recognize them and could have seized the opportunity to exact revenge.

Again, Joseph chose betterment and gave his brothers all that they needed. By the time he revealed himself to them, they were so afraid and thought that he would pay them back in their evil coin. But being a wise man who knew the power of betterment over bitterness, he simply looked on the bright side and encouraged his brothers to do same. Hear him: **"Do not be afraid, for am I in the place of God? But as for you, you meant evil against me; but God meant it for good, in order to bring it about as it is this day, to save many people alive. Now therefore, do not be afraid; I will provide for you and your little ones." And he comforted them and spoke kindly to them."** (Genesis 15:19-21).

# YEMI OYINKANSOLA

## TAUNTED BUT UNDAUNTED

You know Hannah, right? She was one of the most popular women in Bible history. Hannah was one woman who had every cause to be bitter against God, her co-wife, Peninnah, even the priest, Eli, but not once does the Bible mention that she was bitter toward anybody.

Now, as if it wasn't bad enough that Hannah was childless in a crowded marriage (polygamy), her rival, Peninnah, made sure she didn't hear the last of it. Being the second wife, Peninnah wasn't just jealous of Hannah's position in Elkanah's home, she also couldn't bear the fact that she (Hannah) received more attention and affection from their husband. So, she made it her life's goal to provoke and torment Hannah.

Hannah, we were told was very dissatisfied about her childlessness, such that nothing, not even her husband's undying love for her and constant reassurance of that love did much to cheer her up. She wanted children so badly. Pulpit's commentary tries to explain why Elkanah couldn't have been better to Hannah than ten sons. "The husband really is not 'better than ten sons,' for the joy of motherhood is quite distinct from that of conjugal affection, and especially to a Hebrew woman, who had special hopes from which she was cut off by barrenness." This coupled with Peninnah's constant provocation, as the certified pain in the neck that she was, further plunged Hannah into misery and deep sorrow of heart, but not bitterness.

Hannah was neither mad at God for restraining her from bearing children, nor was she resentful towards Peninnah, who she could easily have dealt with by pitching their husband against her and her children. If Hannah had some grouse against God, she won't be consistently seen at the temple during the Jewish annual retreat, making supplications to God.

But how did she manage this? How could she go through such experience and not feel a little something against God? Chapter 2 of 1 Samuel reveals that Hannah was one woman who knew the God she served. She knew that the God of Abraham, Isaac and Jacob wasn't a God that could be pushed around or emotionally blackmailed into taking an action.

He does what He will, whenever He pleases. **He is the one that "killeth, and maketh alive: he bringeth down to the grave, and bringeth up. The LORD maketh poor, and maketh rich: he bringeth low, and lifteth up"** (1 Samuel 2:6-7). All these He does at His own time. So, wisdom taught Hannah to humble herself, trust in God's providence and His promises, hence she patiently waited for Him. And at the time appointed, He visited her.

There at the altar of prayer, making her supplication, the way she knew how, Hannah was again tried. Priest Eli mistook her for a drunk. That was totally unfair. At this point, Hannah had every right to feel irritated, touchy and entitled. "The priest should know better. He should be more sensitive," some of us would have been quick to observe. But Hannah, who knew what she really wanted, refused to fall into that trap.

**"And Hannah answered and said, No, my lord, I am a woman of a sorrowful spirit: I have drunk neither wine nor strong drink, but have poured out my soul before the Lord. Count not thine handmaid for a daughter of Belial: for out of the abundance of my complaint and grief have I spoken hitherto"** (1 Samuel 1:15-16).

Thank God that Hannah made a choice to turn her burden into a reason to pray and not a cause for bitterness and maliciousness. Eli was so touched by her calm response and courteous attitude that he gave a powerful priestly backing to her petition. The result was that she immediately received a strong assurance that her prayer had been answered.

**"Then Eli answered and said, Go in peace: and**

**the God of Israel grant thee thy petition that thou hast asked of him. And she said, Let thine handmaid find grace in thy sight. So the woman went her way, and did eat, and her countenance was no more sad"** (verses 17-18).

Soon after, Hannah became the mother of Samuel, one of the greatest prophets in Israel.

What if Hannah had allowed bitterness to turn her into a jealous, grumpy and faithless woman? She might have considered her attitude justifiable but she would have only ended up missing her time of divine visitation and ended her life as a frustrated childless woman. Indeed, it pays to choose betterment over bitterness!

## A REJECT BECOMES A RESCUER

If there was anyone who had a good reason to hold a bitter grudge, it was Jephthah. Imagine walking down the street, and people point at you, and in fierce whispers to themselves and to your hearing, they mock, "son of a prostitute" or "oh there goes the bastard, what's he up to now?" That was the story of Jephthah.

He was born by a prostitute and hated by his stepmother and brothers who eventually drove him out of his father's house. **"And Gilead's wife bare him sons; and his wife's sons grew up, and they thrust out Jephthah, and said unto him, Thou shalt not inherit in our father's house; for thou art the son of a strange woman.** Then Jephthah fled from his brethren, and dwelt in the land of Tob: and there were gathered vain men to Jephthah, and went out with him" (Judges 11:2-3).

Commenting on the story of Jephthah, David Legge noted, "How many times has this story been repeated in history? Imagine it. A child is born under some cloud of shame or into a dysfunctional family, and as they grow that cloud seems to hover over them and grow larger and larger, and others delight in pointing out its presence over their heads and reminding them of their shameful past. There are many like that in our society today, because of the nature of their birth and the prejudice that comes with it, they aren't given a chance in their family or in the general society. They are rejected without trial by those around them..."

It is common for the people who fall into this category to do what Jephthah did, which was to run away (Judges 11:3). Some, in trying to escape from it all, turn into hard drugs, violence, cultism, prostitution and what have you. They constantly remind themselves how angry they are. They are mad at God, their parents and the society at large. They think there's nothing to live for. Even Jephthah was said to have joined himself with some vain men; but then, he still had the God consciousness. He developed himself as a warrior and as a historian. This was evident in his attempted negotiations with the Ammonites.

Jephthah didn't live the rest of his life feeling mad at his world; rather he made himself so valuable that the elders of Israel came, cap-in-hand, begging him to help them confront the Ammonites in battle. In exchange for this, he was to rule over them for the rest of his life. The rejected now became the elected.

So what's your excuse for indulging in all those vices? You may probably say "God is against me! My family hates me! I'm unfortunate!" But you have two options. You can remain in that self-trap of bitterness and end up in ruin or you can decide to make the most of your situation, by acquainting yourself with your Maker, forgiving the past and preparing yourself for a great opportunity yet to come.

## STEADFAST IN AFFLICTIONS

"Curse God and die," the woman said in frustration. Job looked at his wife and wondered how foolish she could get. Seriously befuddled, Job quipped, **"Shall**

**we receive good at the hand of God, and shall we not receive evil?"** (Job 2:10). He couldn't understand what had come over his wife, with whom he had loved and served God all these years.

Here was a righteous man who ensured that he did everything by the precepts of God, yet he lost everything (his children, wealth, health and even His friends). All that Job had left was his life and integrity. How could God allow such calamity to happen to a man like job?

As if to add salt to injury, his friends were determined to convict him of some sort of secret sins. Job despaired unto death. But in all of these, he held on firmly to his righteous stance. He would not curse God, as his wife counseled. No. he wasn't bitter against God. He had no reason to be. He understood the prerogative to give and take back belonged to God alone. He didn't even see the devil as being the one against him.

When his wife tried to turn his heart against God, he was said to have rebuked her sharply. But, Scriptures never did say that he took a bitter stance against her. His friends likewise, he was not bitter toward them.

In the end, God changed his situation. Everything Job lost was restored to him. And you know what? The Bible says that all of these things started happening when he prayed for his friends. **"And the Lord turned the captivity of Job, when he prayed for his friends: also the Lord gave Job twice as much as he had before"** (Job 42:10).

What situation are you currently? I'm sure it's not worse than that of Job. Look, it's human to feel like God has forsaken you, it's okay to cry and vent, Job felt that way too, but you need to move past you frustration like he did. Take on this Job's never-say-die attitude, **"Though he slay me, yet will I trust in him: but I will maintain mine own ways before him"** (Job 13:15). And God will come through for you as He did Job. He will restore all you have lost, vindicate you and make you a living testimony of His greatness.

## HE PASSED THE TEST!

Here is one person who really knew how to escape the trap of bitterness. Hezekiah had been really sick; then came prophet Isaiah with a message of death, instead of a message of hope and recovery. I can just imagine this happening to any of us today. We might have taken it up with Isaiah for being the bearer of such unpleasant news. But Hezekiah didn't do that; rather he **"turned his face to the wall, and prayed unto the LORD, saying, I beseech thee, O LORD,** remember now how I have walked before thee in truth and with a perfect heart, and have done that which is good in thy sight. And Hezekiah wept sore" (2 Kings 20:2-3).

Someone said, "This is one of the most intriguing incidents in the Bible. Anyone who has passed through a terrible illness and has stared death in the face can relate to this story of Hezekiah and his prayer."

It is during moments like this that you will understand that the name of the Lord is indeed a strong tower that the righteous can run into and be saved. It is moments like this that make you realize how frail we all are and that God, like the Psalmist puts it, is the only strength of our lives. Moments like this cannot be wasted on grudges, resentments and bitterness; only trust in God's love and faithfulness takes a man through a situation like this.

What if after Hezekiah had received the news, he had spent all the time raving and ranting about God's unfaithfulness and prophet Isaiah's insensitivity? What if he had called a pity party and they had started consoling him and further fanning the embers of indignation against God and His prophet? Didn't a man who had served God in truth all his life deserve to be angry if God said he would die, when he was busy waiting on Him for healing?

Hezekiah didn't as much as answer Isaiah a word. He faced God immediately. I don't know what the distance between Hezekiah's bedchamber and the middle court was like. But his prayer reached heaven before Isaiah covered the distance. Prayer reaches God faster than bitter complaints do. God is not moved by tantrums. He is moved by prayers based on His promises. Hezekiah understood this and employed it. Did it work for him? Certainly.

Right before the prophet left the premises of Hezekiah's house, God issued an express command to him, **"Turn again, and tell Hezekiah the captain of my people, Thus saith the LORD, the God of David thy father, I have heard thy prayer, I have seen thy tears: behold, I will heal thee: on the third day thou shalt go up unto the house of the LORD. And I will add unto thy days fifteen years; and I will deliver thee and this city out of the hand of the king of Assyria; and I will defend this city for mine own sake, and for my servant David's sake. And Isaiah said, Take a lump of figs. And they took and laid it on the boil, and he recovered"** (verses 5-7).

# YEMI OYINKANSOLA

## SHE REAPED THE BENEFITS OF BETTERMENT

Joyce Meyer is a household name in the Christendom today. She is well known for her uplifting messages through her regular broadcasts and manifold publications. Having had a fair share of abuse and disappointment in life, she had good reasons to be a bitter person, and of course she was bitter for a time, but did come out of it.

To use her words, "Forgiving someone isn't easy. Believe me, I know from personal experience! But I also know that it is possible. With promises found in scriptures like Philippians 4:13, we can do whatever we need to do with God's power.

Joyce once narrated how her father sexually abused her from the time she was about three years old until she was eighteen. She left home as soon as she could and carried bitterness and unforgiveness in her heart for years.

But over time, as she studied God's word, God began to reveal how harmful it is to live with unforgiveness and the benefits of forgiveness. In her words, "I think sometimes people believe forgiveness is more about doing a favor for the person who hurt them, when actually you are doing yourself a big favor. But the truth is, it is because as you release the bitterness and anger in your heart, you are able to live with real peace and joy."

Joyce allowed God to have His way in her and He healed her of the hurts and the pains she had endured. The root of bitterness was removed and she became totally free – but not just free; she also became empowered and equipped to help others deal with similar situations. Now she has become a renowned speaker, bestselling author, and popular mentor to millions of people worldwide. In other words, she has successfully chosen to let the pains of her past turn her to a much better person today.

Here is her counsel to those struggling with unforgiveness: "You may be thinking, "Okay, Joyce, I want to forgive, but it's so hard. I don't know if I can do it!" Well, I want to encourage you to know that in Christ, you can forgive–no matter what has been done to you."

The examples we have considered so far have indeed confirmed that the decision to be better and not bitter is a choice anyone can make. None of the people mentioned above claimed that it was easy deciding for betterment, but as far as choices were concerned, it was the wisest choice available to them.

Choosing to stay bitter, no matter the cause of your bitterness will only make you more miserable. Deciding for betterment instead of bitterness is for your own good more than it is for the person you are forgiving. You can choose, like the catalogue of examples we have seen, to forget the past and move on to betterment.

## PRAYER POINTS

1. Lord, like all these examples, I choose to come out of every situation better and not bitter. Help me so to do.

2. Give me the grace to manifest your love and mercy towards my offenders

3. Jesus, I pray for grace to keep looking up to you and forward to a better tomorrow. No rolling in the dung. No living in the past.

## CHAPTER 6

# DEALING WITH THE ROOTS OF BITTERNESS

◇◇◇◇◇◇◇◇◇◇◇◇◇◇◇◇◇◇◇◇◇◇◇◇◇◇◇◇◇◇◇◇◇◇◇◇◇◇◇◇◇◇◇◇

So, having realized that it is very possible to choose betterment over bitterness – and that it actually pays to do so, judging by all the numerous examples we have considered, the question is: How exactly does one eliminate bitterness from the heart?

I think there is a straightforward answer to this. The most effective way to kill a plant or weed is to dig it up and destroy the root. That is the same way to deal with bitterness in an individual's life. You need to pull the source of your bitterness out of its hiding place. Expose it and give it to God who alone knows how to cultivate the heart and help you bring forth fruits of righteousness.

There is no alternative to this. The ultimate remedy for bitterness is forgiveness. As one writer puts it, "Forgiveness alone enables you to let go of grievances, grudges, rancor and resentment. It is the single most potent antidote for the venomous desire for retributive justice poisoning your system. And if this impulse hasn't infested you physically, it has at least afflicted you mentally and emotionally. So learning—with or without loving compassion—to forgive your "violator" facilitates your recovering from a wound that, while it may have originated from outside yourself, has been kept alive (and even "nurtured") from the venom you've synthesized within you."

What is forgiveness? The American Psychological Association rightly defines it as "the renunciation or cessation of resentment, indignation or anger as a result of a perceived offense, disagreement, or mistake, or ceasing to demand punishment or restitution."

Max Lucado, in explaining the rationale for forgiveness, says "To forgive someone is to admit our limitations. We've been given only one piece of life's jigsaw puzzle. Only God has the cover of the box. To forgive someone is to display reverence. Forgiveness is not saying the one who hurt you was right. Forgiveness is stating that God is fair and He will do what is right."

If forgiveness is the only way out of bitterness, it then means that what other ways there are will only make you languish in bitterness for as long as you allow. Unless you choose forgiveness, you'll always feel the need to have your own pound of flesh, take vengeance for something wrongly done to you. But then, why choose vengeance? Don't you have enough things to do without trying to do God's work too?

Yes, the business of vengeance is exclusively God's prerogative, for His word says in Romans 12:19, **"Dearly beloved, avenge not yourselves, but rather give place unto wrath: for it is written, Vengeance is mine; I will repay, saith the Lord."**

So, there you have read it yourself. Leave vengeance to God. Truly, people deserve to pay for their sins. We all do. But then, it is God's prerogative to visit vengeance on those who so deserve it. Let go and let God.

How then do you deal with the root of bitterness and be completely free from it?

## ACKNOWLEDGMENT IS CRUCIAL

Bitterness cannot be dealt with unless you first admit that you have the bitter root. More often than not, people who have the bitter root do not even know it is there. You'll recall that in describing bitterness in the opening chapter, I did note that it is unnoticeable to the human eyes, except through its fruits.

So, once it becomes obvious that the bitter root resides in you, you must acknowledge that it's really there. The road to recovery opens up from this point of acknowledgement.

## BE WILLING TO BE HEALED

It isn't enough just to acknowledge, you must open your heart to recovery. Let me explain. If an individual is sick and visits the doctor, he acknowledges that he is sick, which is why he goes to the doctor in the first place. But if for whatever reason, say to abdicate responsibilities at work or home, this individual wants to lay sick for a while, he will deliberately choose not to take the medication given him by that doctor. So, even though he has visited the doctor in acknowledgement of his sick state, he is not ready for recovery and will not recover until he takes his medications.

The same goes for becoming free from bitterness. While acknowledgement is vital to the healing process, there is also the place of conscious willingness to let go of the hurts, disappointments, abuse, and also release the perpetrators. One thing that should help you in doing this has already been repeatedly emphasized – bitterness, like poison, hurts the carrier much more than the supposed target.

After you must have opened your heart to receive healing that comes only from God, then you must begin to identify the source of your bitterness.

## IDENTIFY THE SOURCE AND OBJECT OF YOUR BITTERNESS

You must try and identify what is responsible for your bitterness and the person at whom the bitterness is directed. These two go hand-in-glove. Was your bitterness caused by abuse, deprivation, disappointment, disaster, natural or manmade? Is it directed at humanity or divinity? The ability to identify the source and object of your bitterness is one big step in the direction of recovery.

Bitterness, as you must know is often directed at something. It could be towards humanity (oneself and others) or divinity (God). And of course, it could be toward unpalatable circumstance. This last one is invariably linked to the first and second, for if an individual's bitterness is directed at a war that wiped out her entire family, it may very well be that the real object of her bitterness isn't exactly the war, but the enemies that killed her family, if she identified them, and the supernatural powers that 'did nothing to save them.'

Let us get a little practical here. How do you deal with bitterness toward God? The following steps, as suggested by a Christian author, may help.

## 1. Trust God's wisdom

This doesn't mean you should believe that everything that happens on earth is good. Sin is in the world. Satan is still the prince of the air. Yet you must believe that God allows things to happen that He may not like, and which we may not like. But in His wisdom, somewhere down the line, God will turn it around for good for His children, according to His promise in Romans 8:28.

## 2. Get the lessons in it

Second, you have to ask God what He's trying to teach you through this. Everything we go through in life happens for us to learn a lesson or two. Know that nothing ever happens without the knowledge of God, and that if He permits certain events, there definitely would be a lesson or two He wants us to learn from such experiences. So, when things happen and you are tempted to be bitter toward God, take a moment's pause and ask Him what lessons are embedded in that challenge.

## 3. Stand on God's promises

Third, apply one of God's promises to your situation. There is a promise in God's word for every situation. Instead of continuing to wallow in bitterness, why not check out God's word and find that promise that better suits your situation. And let that promise reassure you of God's abiding faithfulness, your challenges notwithstanding.

## 4. Don't allow self-pity

Fourth, reject self-pity. It gets you nowhere, but keeps you moving anyway. Take off and burn up the garb of self-pity. Nothing you're going through is peculiar to you alone. Let's even say it is; wallowing in self-pity only makes it impossible for you to get out of that unpleasant predicament. So, shun self-pity.

## 5. Use your time wisely

Fifth, put time into proper perspective. Time, they say, heals all wounds. It doesn't matter what you're going through at the moment, time is what it takes to heal up. So, that difficult situation only needs time to either get better or worse, depending on what you do. Sink deep into bitterness and the situation gets worse; or snap out of bitterness and get better insight on how to make the best of the situation.

## 6. Thanksgiving and thanks living

Sixth, be quick to give thanks. I love a word someone coined recently, 'thanks living.' This is you not just having an attitude of gratitude. It is you living thanks, living gratitude. Being thankful is second nature to you. When you begin to live thanks, then bitterness will have no place in you. A thankful heart is a joyful heart. Tell me how bitterness can thrive there? Moreover, can you be thankful to God and be bitter toward Him at the same time?

So, what if you're bitter at yourself? How many times have you done things and you just couldn't stop browbeating yourself? The regret and guilt just won't go away. You can't forgive yourself for failing to strap your baby in her car seat, which was why you lost her to the accident. Maybe your failure to service the car led to an accident that led to the loss of innocent lives, or someone got fired at work as a result of your ineptitude or whatever. You just can't forgive yourself for whatever it is. How do you deal with that?

Begin by confessing your faults to the Lord, and believing His promise of His faithfulness and justice in forgiving all your sins, as 1 John 1:9 tells us. But then, it is not automatic that after you have confessed your sins, the weight and guilt of that sin immediately disappears. The devil is always on the side to remind you of your 'worthlessness' every time. But you must, in childlike faith, believe that God has indeed forgiven you and you have no reason not to forgive yourself.

Look at it this way. Your little boy has just disobeyed you and got scolded or spanked, depending on the gravity of the offense. You explained to him why you had to scold or spank him, made him promise not to repeat the action, and gave him a reassuring hug that he had been forgiven. It is dinner time, and your boy who has always had a healthy appetite is busy picking at his meal. You can't understand, so you ask. And he says, "Mum, I still feel terrible for what I did earlier."

You can relate with that, can't you? That's exactly what you do when you are bitter at yourself. Even though you have received the forgiveness of God and that of others, whom you have offended, you don't find the strength to forgive yourself.

There's no shortcut to forgiving yourself. Just let the guilt go. Don't let the enemy mess up with your mind. He's very good at that, should you allow him. If you can forgive those who offend you, then you don't have to be unnecessarily hard on yourself. From the graciousness of your heart, you must forgive yourself.

## YOU MAY SEEK THE HELP OF A GODLY COUNSELOR

Yes, sometimes, there may be need to seek the help of a godly counselor. This counselor may be your pastor in church, an elderly neighbor, who is a mature believer in Christ, your Sunday school teacher, or anyone to whom you look up.

You understand why it may be necessary for you to seek the help of a counselor? Talking about your bitterness to someone who understands you will more likely help you out of bitterness faster than trying by yourself. It's even possible that this individual may have at one time or the other had to deal with the bitter root in their life, and so it makes them better poised to help you out of it through godly counsel.

In choosing who to talk to, however, you must be careful not to fall into the wrong hands. It will be impossible for you to deal with bitterness if your counselor decides to take the stance of a pity party. While, it is okay to empathize with you, as that helps in a way to eliminate the feelings of guilt and condemnation, taking sides with you and cutting down your offenders will only make the healing process more difficult.

If you ever have the opportunity to counsel someone who is consumed by bitterness and a vengeful spirit, then you must prayerfully carry out that counseling, and resist the temptation to be drawn into that person's bitterness in a bid to be empathetic with him or her.

## REALIZE THAT BITTERNESS IS A SIN THAT MUST BE REPENTED OF

This also is a crucial approach in dealing with bitterness. When you realize that bitterness (regardless of the cause) is a sin against God, it helps you to be more eager to deal with it. Ephesians 4:31 says it clearly: **"Let all bitterness, and wrath, and anger, and clamor, and evil speaking, be put away from you, with all malice."**

See, it doesn't matter whether we all try to justify it by calling it a medical condition or an innate thing, bitterness is sin before God. Full stop!

So, how do you deal with sin? The Bible makes it clear that God hates sin, and that sin can rob you of spending eternity with God in heaven. In the light of these revelations, how should you deal with sin? You must hate sin. Bitterness is sin. Hate it. When you come to that point in your life where bitterness repulses you, it will become easier to deal with it. There's no way you can continue to live with something that you loathe.

As you begin to loathe bitterness, you will discover that you will begin to seek ways to be rid of it. At this point, you must turn to God. Tell Him you're aware that you've been living in rebellion against Him and that you're most willing to make a right turn. Now, confess your sin of bitterness that you have for so long held on to. Ask for grace to forgive all offenders and grace never to relapse into bitterness again. God, who is faithful and just to forgive sins, will hear your cry and deliver you from the sin of bitterness. It is possible.

James J. Messina's five-step plan of dealing with bitterness is apt in summing up the thrust of this chapter:

- Identify the source of your bitterness and what this person did to evoke your resentful feelings;

- Develop a new way of looking at your past, present, and future—including how resentment has negatively affected your life and how letting go of it can improve your future;

- Write a letter to this person, describing [their] offenses toward you, then forgive and let go of them (but don't send the letter) [Note, by the way, that choosing to renew your tie to the individual who seriously offended you is totally separate from your choice to forgive them];

- Visualize your having a better future, having neutralized the negative impact of resentment; and

- If bitter, resentful feelings remain, return to Step 1 and begin again. [For it may be only through diligently repeating this process many times that you can at last forgo the almost instinctual drive (if only in your thoughts) toward retribution and revenge].

## PRAYER POINTS

1. Lord, it has become clear that bitterness is sin against you. I repent of all bitterness and ask for grace never to relapse into it.

2. Lord, help me through the process of dealing with bitterness in my heart.

3. Strengthen me to let go of hurts and so that your Spirit can have His way in my life and affairs.

*CHAPTER 7*

# DOMINION OVER BITTERNESS

◇◇◇◇◇◇◇◇◇◇◇◇◇◇◇◇◇◇◇◇◇◇◇◇◇◇◇◇◇◇◇◇◇◇◇◇◇◇

Have you ever had a weight taken off your shoulders? I don't mean literarily now. Have you ever had a longstanding need met, or finally executed a project you'd been on for so long? Have you ever sorted out a problem that had for long gnawed at you? Do you recall the overwhelming peace that settled over you? The peace that settles upon your heart and mind when the root of bitterness is thoroughly dealt with may very well be that overwhelming peace you experience when a heavy burden is lifted off you.

But then, after you have successfully dealt with the root of bitterness, how do you ensure that you're not yoked by it again? Apostle Paul, in his letter to the Galatians, charged, **"Stand fast therefore in the liberty wherewith Christ hath made us free, and be not entangled again with the yoke of bondage"** (Galatians 5:1).

How then can we ensure that we are not again plagued by the root of bitterness after we must have been made free from it?

## 1. Accept that Offenses Must Come

One of the realities of life is that things can't always go our way, and people can't always act towards us the way we expect them to. Individuals are different, based on backgrounds, upbringing, personal experiences, level of education and exposure, as well as temperament and level of maturity. These differences go a long way in influencing people's behaviors.

This is why Jesus Christ makes it clear to us that we cannot live without offenses in the world. He says it clearly in Luke 17:1, **"It is impossible that no offenses should come..."** Armed with this knowledge, it should be a lot easier to deal with offenses and offenders.

To further explore the issue of offenses, it is important to be mindful of the following reasons why people may come:

- The selfish nature of your offender. Some people do certain things, not with the intention to hurt you, but for their own selfish gains. That's right! The unregenerate human nature is such that it seeks its own. And only people who have come to understand the essence of living beyond selfish gains truly understand that pursuing personal gains at the expense of another person's happiness can bring hurt to that person.

- Inability of your offender to handle life's challenges. Often times, people are overwhelmed by their troubles, so much so that they snap at everything and everybody. This person who is weighed down by events in his life may be a loved one. Naturally, it is the people closest to him that receive the heat of his frustrations. So, many times, people hurt you not because they just feel like it, but because they have not learnt to put a rein on their emotions to avoid unnecessary outbursts when they are overwhelmed by too much to do or the troubles of this life.

- A reaction to something you did. No doubt, it is better to respond to situations, actions of people rather than react. But then, not everyone has the ability so to do. Some people react very quickly to actions they find disturbing. So, it is possible that someone will be unkind to you because that person had first perceived you as being unkind. And because you don't bother to ask what informed the person's behavior, you go ahead and ruminate on what he had done to offend you, until your mind begins to justify the reason for your bitterness.

Of course, we cannot exactly rule out the fact that some people intentionally set out to hurt others. There are those who, for reasons that you just can't ascertain, seem to derive pleasure in making you angry or sad. Whatever the case is, however, it is up to you to fortify yourself emotionally and through the grace and word of God, so that no fiery darts that can cause bitterness is allowed in your heart.

One potent way of dealing with offenses is mentioned in Ephesians 4:26: **"Be ye angry and sin not. Let not the sun go down upon your wrath."** What this suggests is that, while getting offended may be inevitable, you must endeavor to keep your anger under check, so as to ensure that it doesn't linger for longer than is necessary. If someone offends you, it is better you settle it before the day runs out. Failure to settle matters as they arise, whether between spouses, friends, brethren, colleagues, will make such matters escalate.

If someone says something that makes you angry for instance, it is better to let that person know that what he or she said made you unhappy. Whether they apologize or not, let it go once you express your mind. Sleeping over the matter will most likely cause your anger to fester, and it is most likely that you'll be angrier or even bitter by the morning. So, deal with you anger before dusk.

## 2. Be a "Peace Addict"

Resolve to be a man or woman of peace, regardless of the circumstances. God's word counsels us to **"Seek peace and pursue it"** (Psalms 34:14). And this has to be a personal decision, even if certain people choose to be unreasonably difficult. This is why the Bible says it in another place: **"Follow peace with ALL men…"** (Hebrews 12:14).

In resisting the root of bitterness, you must earnestly pursue after peace. Ever seen the way a thirsty deer would go after a water brook? It is with that exact passion that you should seek to live at peace with everyone you have to do with.

Suppose someone doesn't greet or respond to your greetings, should you be bitter about that? Come off it! This person, for all you know may not even know you exist. Besides, greeting or response to it is common courtesy, and if someone lacks courtesy, should you then make it your personal problem? Not at all!

Never let your life be dictated by someone's wrong behavior or disappointment, especially when this someone has moved on with his own life. Feel the pain of the disappointment for a while; just don't let it linger for longer than is meet. Let it go; for only in letting go can you find true freedom and real satisfaction in life.

## 3. Realize the Futility Of Bitterness

As we have noted before, every moment spent in bitterness is spent in futility. Bitterness is in itself a futile emotion. When you're bitter against yourself or your fellow man, you dissipate so much energy. And while the feeling of bitterness may make you feel good for a while, it leaves you feeling miserable and alone.

Now, if being bitter against man can do so much damage to you, can you pause for a moment and imagine what choosing to be bitter against God can do to you? It's complete waste of time, energy and emotions to take a bitter stance against the Creator of the ends of the earth.

Someone may say they are bitter against God because of disasters and misfortunes all around. The truth, however, is that being bitter against God will in no way take away the hurt or make them feel better.

Besides, you have to understand that certain things in life will always be beyond your understanding as a human. You cannot try to fathom or change everything in life in conformity to your desires. Even the Bible tells us plainly that **"The secret things belong to the Lord our God, but those things which are revealed belong to us and to our children forever, that we may do all the words of this law"** (Deuteronomy 29:29).

I think this is the more reason why you should make this prayer of Francis Asisi your daily heart cry. "God, grant me the serenity to accept the things I cannot change, courage to change the things I can, and wisdom to know the difference." That is the reality of life – not everything will be within the power of humans to influence or control!

Again, you must resist the temptation to be bitter against God because things don't seem to be working out right for you at the moment. Bear in mind that God cannot be arm-twisted into working things out for you, simply because you are bitter against Him. Bitterness just doesn't change the person of God or His position on a matter. God remains God, whether man is bitter or not.

This is why you must do all you can to stay away from bitterness, whether it is directed at humanity or divinity. Bitterness has helped no one and it never will. The only person who suffers as a result of your bitterness is the carrier.

## 4. Resist the "Entitlement" Mentality

Entitlement mentality or complex is the belief that the world owes you something. It is a state of mind in which someone is constantly looking to others to do something for them rather than focusing on what they can do for themselves. You must understand that, in reality, nobody in this life owes you anything. The earlier you accept this, the easier it will be for you to handle disappointments. Don't carry on your life expecting the whole world to be at your beck and call. It is a good thing for people to offer this assistance or that, but that's just what it is, assistance, a favor, privilege, not a right.

## 5. Understand that Everything You Have is From God

Maybe you don't get bitter because people are not nice to you. But maybe you are tempted to become bitter because people do not reciprocate your kind gestures? Of course, it can be painful when people don't seem to acknowledge or appreciate the good deeds you have done to them. But here is a way of thinking that should cheer you up a bit. Everything you have, in the first place, belongs to God; and when you give to others, you're actually acknowledging God's ownership of all you've achieved and at the same time obeying His commandment to good. Consequently, the reward of your good deeds is bound to come from God Himself. This is why the Bible says that **"He that hath pity upon the poor lendeth unto the Lord; and that which he hath given will he pay him again"** (Proverbs 19:17).

But beyond that, Jesus specifically tells us the motive with which we must help and do good to others in Luke 6:32-36: **"For if ye love them which love you, what thank have ye? for sinners also love those that love them. And if ye do good to them which do good to you, what thank have ye? for sinners also do even the same. And if ye lend to them of whom ye hope to receive, what thank have ye? for sinners also lend to sinners, to receive as much again. But love ye your enemies, and do good, and lend, hoping for nothing again; and your reward shall be great, and ye shall be the children of the Highest: for he is kind unto the unthankful and to the evil. Be ye therefore merciful, as your Father also is merciful."**

Think about it. The most essential things in life come to us free of charge. Is it the air we breathe? Water? Love and affection? Family and friends? Name it! Imagine you had to pay for the air you breathe; how much money would you have to be able to afford it for a lifetime? God gives freely, and so should you.

**6. Forgive Again**

The Lord Jesus had just given His commands concerning restoring a repentant offender who is of the household of faith. Apparently, this graciousness of unconditional forgiveness the Lord taught somewhat took Peter, and probably the rest of the disciples by surprise. But, since Peter happened to be the most outspoken of them all, he was the one who first found his voice, **"Lord, how often shall my brother sin against me, and I forgive him? Till seven times?" He asked, obviously bemused** (Matthew 18:21).

If Peter had asked the question in an attempt to talk the Master into readjusting His position on the matter, he most certainly received the shock of his life, when Jesus firmly but calmly responded to his question, **"I say not unto thee, Until seven times; but, Until seven times seven"** (Matthew 18:22).

With that response, Jesus wanted to make His hearers understand that forgiveness is limitless. So, even if your brother offends you four times, seven times, or

490 times, you are expected to forgive him readily and fully. Jesus, through His response, made it clear to His hearers, as well as you and me by extension that every time a brother or sister offends you and comes to ask for forgiveness, you shouldn't say, "I forgave you the last time and you've done the same thing repeatedly." Rather, you should extend a full forgiveness for each offense. The grace of God is available for you to do this.

God's word demands that forgiveness should be extended to a brother or sister when he repents. But one time too many, we tend to put ourselves in the position of a judge, and try to determine whether or not our offenders' repentance is real or pretentious. This however is not the issue. Whether or not you perceive your offender's repentance as genuine or otherwise, you are to forgive. Even when your forgiveness isn't solicited, forgive fully and freely in any case.

## 7. Let Love Saturate Your Heart

The Scriptures reveals that love covers a whole lot of sin. When love rules your heart, it will be impossible for bitterness to stay there. Where knowledge fails, love can never fail. You may be wondering what I mean by that. Knowledge and love are two different concepts. Now, you may have the knowledge that holding on to bitterness against anyone is by far worse for you than it is for that individual. Even though you have that knowledge, you may still be bitter. But if you allow the love of God saturate your heart by constantly renewing your mind in the light of His word, it therefore becomes easier to forgive your offenders.

Because of the love you have towards others, you find it extremely difficult to hold a grudge against them. In fact, more often than not, you catch yourself praying for your offenders instead of brooding about what they have done to you. This is the power of the love of God spread abroad in your heart.

## 8. Be Sincere About How You Feel

Don't be in the habit of pretending that something somebody did didn't get to you. Don't make sweeping things under the carpet a norm either. Learn to address issues as they come. If anybody, your spouse, boss, subordinate, friend, pastor, parents, does anything that hurts you, find the most polite way to let them know.

But let me sound this helpful note of warning. Don't tell anyone who has hurt you about what they did to hurt you with the intention of getting an apology. The reason you should (not compulsorily) talk to them is that talking has a way of helping you take off some steam.

Now, you're not to expect any apologies from them because while some may find it difficult apologizing to you, especially those above you, others may have intentionally hurt you, and demanding an apology from them is making yourself more susceptible to their vexation. So, express your hurt with an open mind.

You do know that no one method works for two people, right?. Granted that some people could use some talking to get over a little hurt, others just prefer to be quiet about it and let time heal them, yet others would rather talk to God about that little hurt. Whichever way works for you, just don't let the hurt fester till it becomes something so big it spoils everything.

## 9. Don't Try to Force Every Relationship to Work

Understandably, some people may just choose a hateful stance against you, and no matter what you do to ensure a good relationship with them, all your efforts prove abortive. For such people, you may need to keep your distance and just keep them in your prayers, so that your constant relation with them doesn't ensnare you into the yoke of bitterness from which you have been delivered.

## 10. Don't Just Forgive – Forget!

Is it possible to forget a hurt that runs so deep? Yes. Let me explain. Maybe you may not be able to completely delete memories of bad things done to you from your brain (due to the brain's recording process); but because you don't hold a grudge against your offender, when you do have cause to remember the offense, there isn't a trace of hatred or anger in you towards your offender.

One Christian author in very clear terms explains what it means to forget an offense. "The Bible says God remembers our sins no more. So how can God forget something when He is omniscient? How can He know everything and still forget? Here's the secret: When you forgive and forget, the forgetting means that you, like God, don't hold that wrongdoing to the offender's account. God forgets the charge against us; He remembers it no more. Oh, He knows about it, just as you do, but He will never bring it up again. That's what we are to do. Don't fish in the pond of history. Leave it there."

It was said of Robert E. Lee that after the American Civil War, he visited a home in Kentucky. The lady of the house pointed to a limbless, battered tree trunk standing on the front lawn, and said, "Before the

Union army came through here; that was a beautiful, magnificent magnolia tree. Then they blasted it with their artillery, and that's all that's left. What do you think about that?"

She expected the general to sympathize with her and criticize the Union Army. But instead, he looked at her and said in one sentence: "Cut it down and forget it."

Don't keep blasted trees of offenses standing in your life. Cut them down and forget them. **"Let all bitterness, and wrath, and anger, and clamor, and evil speaking, be put away from you, with all malice: And be ye kind one to another, tenderhearted, forgiving one another, even as God for Christ's sake hath forgiven you"** (Ephesians 4:31-32).

You have read it all and I hope you have been blessed. Bitterness does no good to you, your relationship with God or your fellow men. You can decide for betterment and live a life that is completely free of bitterness by yielding your heart to the Jesus Christ. He will help you uproot that bitter root and give you a new heart saturated with love, such that it will be completely impossible for you to nurse bitterness against anyone ever.

## PRAYER POINTS

1. Dear Father, help me to abide in Your love because only then will I be able to forgive again and again.

2. Lord, I no longer want to be entangled in the web of bitterness, please help me and set me free indeed.

3. Help me to permanently forgive offences of the past just as you forgive and forget my sins.

# THE GREATEST PRAYER OF A LIFETIME

The greatest prayer of a lifetime is to be reconnected back to God in a living relationship. Relationship is the basis for asking. You cannot pray to a God whom you don't know and who does not know you. God wants to be intimate with you. This type of relationship is available to each one of us when we sincerely repent of our sins, ask for God's forgiveness, and receive His Son, Jesus, as our personal Lord and Savior. If you have never surrendered your life to God, or if you have turned away from God and you want to return to Him, now is the time. God is waiting for you. His arms are open wide to receive you. Just pray this simple prayer right now:

O Lord, be merciful to me, a sinner. I realize that I am a sinner. I need a Savior and you are my savior. I repent of every sin, every wrongdoing, and I ask for your forgiveness. I receive Jesus Christ, Your only begotten Son, as my Lord and my Savior. I believe that Jesus went to the cross for me and paid the price for my salvation, and now I receive Him into my heart. I declare that I am born again. I am a child of God. Old sins are gone, and I have a brand-new life in Christ in Jesus' name. Amen.

If you prayed this prayer and wish to contact Pastor Yemi for guidance, please email him at: info@yemioyinkansola.com

# ABOUT PASTOR
## YEMI OYINKANSOLA

Pastor Yemi Oyinkansola, a professional banker called into full time ministry is a teacher and an encourager with deep spiritual insight.

He is a worshipper and a prayer warrior who believes that all things are possible through God when you engaged in intensive worship and fervent prayer through faith.

He Pastors with the Redeemed Christian Church of God in California USA where he resides with his beautiful wife Comfort and two lovely children, Melody and Toluwani.

www.ingramcontent.com/pod-product-compliance
Lightning Source LLC
Chambersburg PA
CBHW070649050426
42451CB00008B/319